POLITIGUIDE 2016

POLITIGUIDE
—— 2016 ——

A Simple and Neutral Summary of the Most
Important Issues in the 2016 Presidential Election

UNDERSTAND THE ISSUES

STAY INFORMED

JOIN THE DISCUSSION

EMPOWER YOURSELF

Julian Rudolph and Kyle Hackel

New York

PolitiGuide 2016

A Simple and Neutral Summary of the Most Important Issues in the 2016
Presidential Election

Understand the Issues • Stay Informed • Join the Discussion • Empower Yourself

Published in New York, New York, by Morgan James Publishing. Morgan James and
The Entrepreneurial Publisher are trademarks of Morgan James, LLC.
www.MorganJamesPublishing.com

The Morgan James Speakers Group can bring authors to your live event. For more
information or to book an event visit The Morgan James Speakers Group at
www.TheMorganJamesSpeakersGroup.com.

Shelfie

A **free** eBook edition is available
with the purchase of this print book.

CLEARLY PRINT YOUR NAME ABOVE IN UPPER CASE

Instructions to claim your free eBook edition:
1. Download the Shelfie app for Android or iOS
2. Write your name in **UPPER CASE** above
3. Use the Shelfie app to submit a photo
4. Download your eBook to any device

ISBN 978-1-63047-706-6 paperback
ISBN 978-1-63047-707-3 eBook
Library of Congress Control Number:
2015911677

Cover Design by:
Rachel Lopez
www.r2cdesign.com

Interior Design by:
Bonnie Bushman
The Whole Caboodle Graphic Design

In an effort to support local communities and raise awareness and funds, Morgan James
Publishing donates a percentage of all book sales for the life of each book to Habitat for
Humanity Peninsula and Greater Williamsburg

Get involved today, visit
www.MorganJamesBuilds.com

TABLE OF CONTENTS

MISSION STATEMENT
AND PURPOSE

What is this book about?

This book summarizes the most important issues in the 2016 Presidential election in an unbiased format. The issues are discussed according to what Democrats and Republicans *generally* believe and the stances that they commonly take on them. We break down the arguments to their most basic level so that they are easy to read and understand. In short, understanding the issues and the most common party-line viewpoints on them will help you understand the election more clearly.

Why is this book important?

Most of us discuss politics—especially during election time. We all have political opinions, whether we're two Senators hammering out the details of a new piece of legislation, college friends debating a controversial topic over a couple of beers, or family members sitting around the kitchen table. But talking politics is often frustrating, confusing and complicated. It's not easy. Why? The truth is that people usually learn about politics in three ways: the news, social media, and by talking to other people. These are not good places to learn about political issues because they are sometimes biased, misleading, or fail to explain the bigger picture—not to mention all of the name calling, attack advertisements, and lies that are part of a Presidential election. The problem is that Americans do not have a source for reliable, unbiased and general political knowledge. That's where *POLITIGUIDE 2016* comes in.

What will this book do for you?

This book gives you, the American voter, a simple, clear and neutral look at the most important political issues of the 2016 Presidential election. It will empower you with information so that you can form sound opinions and perhaps think about the issues in a different way. This book might make you think that your opinions were right all along, or it might make you consider a different perspective. *POLITIGUIDE 2016* compares

Republicans' and Democrats' political viewpoints side-by-side on each issue, and points out areas where the two parties actually agree. This book will equip you with the knowledge to hold your own in a political conversation. And best of all, you'll get all of this in less than 50 pages.

What the book is NOT meant to do.

This book was not written to sway you toward one party or the other. It does not contain a list of facts, charts, or data designed to justify either side's viewpoint, nor is it intended to be a summary of how *all* Republicans or *all* Democrats feel about an issue. After reading this book, you will not walk away with vast political knowledge. We do not discuss individual candidates or current elected officials because this book is about political parties and their general viewpoints, not politicians. Once again, the book only explains the key issues and what the two major parties believe in the simplest form possible. To take our pledge of neutrality a step further, we've arranged the issues in alphabetical order to avoid the assumption that some are more important than others.

So without further ado, let's begin our exploration of the key issues up for debate in the 2016 Presidential election.

A SIMPLE AND NEUTRAL
SUMMARY OF THE PARTIES

To make informed decisions in the voting booth in 2016, you'll first need a basic understanding of the two major political parties operating in the United States today: the Democrats and the Republicans. Of course there are many other parties too, such as the Libertarians, the Socialists, the Communist Party, and so on. It seems as if there's a party out there representing almost every interest you can imagine. There's the Green Party for people concerned with the environment. There's the Prohibition Party for folks opposed to the sale and consumption of alcohol. There's even a Pirate Party (Google it; it's not what you think) and a Marijuana Party (no need to Google that one; it IS what you think).

Nonetheless, we have chosen to focus *POLITIGUIDE 2016* exclusively on the Democrats and Republicans for two reasons. First, it would take a book of encyclopedic proportions to report on today's most pressing issues through the unique lenses of all the different parties in America. None of us has that kind of time. Second, the last President who was neither a Democrat nor a Republican took office more than 150-years ago—Millard Fillmore of the now-defunct Whig Party in 1850—and Democrats and Republicans have dominated Presidential elections in America ever since. It's a safe bet that they will continue their domination into 2016 as well.

Therefore, let's get a quick snapshot of what these two parties stand for, because knowing their basic philosophies and ideals will help you better understand the candidates they nominate to run for President.

THE DEMOCRATS

The symbol of the Democratic Party is the donkey, and its theme color is blue. Democrats are often called *liberals*, and are also known as being on *the left* of the political spectrum.

Generally speaking, Democrats believe that government should play a starring role in ensuring fairness, justice, and progression in society. The party promotes the notion of *societal responsibility*, meaning that the community (as represented by its government) has the obligation to ensure that everyone living within it has an equal opportunity to succeed and to achieve a certain standard of living. They propose doing this by means of social programs such as welfare, food stamps, and housing assistance (often called "safety nets") and through educational and training opportunities and access to free or low-cost healthcare.

From an economic standpoint, Democrats believe that the government should regulate business, commerce and the economy to ensure that no company, sector or industry oversteps its bounds. To pay for social programs that benefit the poor, they favor higher tax rates for those in the upper tax brackets. This is sometimes called *redistribution of wealth*. They also support a higher federally-mandated minimum wage.

Prominent past Presidents from the Democratic Party are:

- Barack Obama
- Bill Clinton
- Lyndon B. Johnson
- John F. Kennedy
- Harry Truman
- Franklin D. Roosevelt
- Andrew Jackson

Blue States—meaning those whose population cast more votes for the Democratic candidate—from the 2012 Presidential election were:

- California
- Colorado
- Connecticut
- Delaware
- District of Columbia
- Florida
- Hawaii
- Illinois
- Iowa
- Maine
- Maryland
- Massachusetts
- Michigan
- Minnesota
- Nevada
- New Hampshire
- New Jersey
- New Mexico
- New York
- Ohio
- Oregon
- Pennsylvania
- Rhode Island
- Vermont
- Virginia
- Washington
- Wisconsin

The Republicans

The symbol of the Republican Party is the elephant, and its theme color is red. Republicans are often called *conservatives*, and are also known as being on *the right* of the political spectrum. The party goes by the nickname The GOP, which is short for The Grand Old Party.

Generally speaking, Republicans believe that the government's size and role should be limited so as not to obstruct business or infringe on individual rights. The party promotes the notion of *individual responsibility*, meaning that they believe people should be free to live their lives and make decisions on their own terms, without government intrusion.

They believe that with all the opportunities present in America, whether a person succeeds or fails is entirely up to them.

From an economic standpoint, Republicans believe that government should maintain a hand-off approach to business and commerce, which they sometimes refer to as *the free market*. They favor a lower tax burden for everyone, arguing that as long as the government's size and role in society is limited—as they propose—then higher tax rates are unnecessary.

Prominent past Presidents from the Republican Party are:

- George W. Bush
- George H.W. Bush
- Ronald Reagan
- Richard Nixon
- Dwight D. Eisenhower
- Theodore Roosevelt
- Abraham Lincoln

Red States—meaning those whose population cast more votes for the Republican candidate—from the 2012 Presidential election were:

Alabama	Montana
Alaska	Nebraska
Arizona	North Carolina
Arkansas	North Dakota
Georgia	Oklahoma
Idaho	South Carolina
Indiana	South Dakota
Kansas	Tennessee
Kentucky	Texas
Louisiana	Utah
Mississippi	West Virginia
Missouri	Wyoming

A SIMPLE AND NEUTRAL
SUMMARY OF THE ISSUES

Just about any topic is ripe for debate in the months leading up to a Presidential election. In past campaigns, the candidates have debated the pros and cons of stem cell research, flag burning, states' rights, school prayer, crime prevention, affirmative action, free trade, and nuclear arms, just to name a few. There have even been debates about family values, and what it means to be a "real American."

What follows are explanations of several of the important issues that are likely to get the candidates talking as we march toward Election Day 2016. Take a look and see which viewpoints most closely align with your own and which ones challenge you to rethink your current opinion. Do your best to keep an open mind.

To stay up-to-date on the candidates' stances on these issues, we encourage you to read news reports from a variety of sources, listen to the candidates' speeches, watch the party conventions, and tune in to the debates. You might be pleasantly surprised by how interesting (and occasionally, downright entertaining) it is to watch a Presidential campaign unfold.

ABORTION

*This section discusses religious views,
personal choice, and morality*

Brief History of the Issue

An abortion is when a woman intentionally terminates her pregnancy resulting in the death of the unborn child. Abortion is currently legal in the United States. The Supreme Court ruled in the landmark case *Roe v. Wade* (1976) that women have the right to privacy, which includes the right to have an abortion. However, the court ruled that the government can intervene when the fetus has matured beyond a certain point (during the third trimester). The most commonly debated issue here is whether human life begins at conception (when a man's sperm joins with a woman's egg cell), when the baby is born, or at some point in between. The *Roe v. Wade* decision was highly controversial at the time, and remains so to this day. From it, two main viewpoints on abortion emerged that have been adopted by Republicans and Democrats.

Republican Stance

Generally, Republicans take the "pro-life" position on abortion. Pro-life supporters argue that killing an innocent human being is wrong. In their eyes, an unborn fetus is an innocent human being. Republicans often argue that life begins at conception, and that every human being has the fundamental right to life. Some Republicans base this view on the words of the Declaration of Independence, which states:

> *All men are created equal, that they are endowed by their creator with certain inalienable rights, that among these rights are Life, Liberty, and the pursuit of Happiness.*

The argument is that abortion takes these rights away from an unborn child. Republicans and anti-abortion groups also argue that fetuses feel pain during the abortion procedure. Although scientific data is not entirely conclusive as to when and if a fetus may feel pain, some argue that fetuses feel pain as early as the first trimester.

Democratic Stance

Democrats often take the "pro-choice" position on abortion. These supporters generally believe that life begins after birth, not at conception, and that fetuses do not feel pain when most abortions are performed. Similarly, many Democrats argue that a mother has the right to choose whether or not she wants to have an abortion. In short, the choice is hers to make, not the government's or anyone else's. They support this notion with the Supreme Court's ruling in *Roe v. Wade*. Supreme Court Justice Sandra Day O'Connor summarized a popular pro-choice stance in 1992 when she said:

> *The ability of women to participate equally in the economic and social life of the Nation has been facilitated by their ability to control their reproductive lives.*

Pro-choice supporters also argue that a woman should not be forced to have a baby when she is impregnated after being raped. On this point, many Republicans agree. Similarly, Democrats and Republicans sometimes agree that women should not be forced to have a child with known birth defects.

Capital Punishment

This section discusses crime prevention and morality

Brief History of the Issue

Capital punishment (also known as the death penalty) is the legal process of executing someone as punishment for committing a crime. In the United States, crimes that can result in the death penalty are known as "capital crimes." Murder most commonly triggers the death penalty. Fifty-eight countries around the world currently use the death penalty in their legal systems, and approximately 140 countries do not. Capital punishment is legal in the United States, but is only practiced in some states.

This is because the Federal government has granted individual states the right to decide if they want to implement capital punishment within their borders or not.

The death penalty issue has been debated all over the world for hundreds of years. Many countries have historically used different forms of the death penalty as punishment for a variety of crimes. In America, the most common execution method is lethal injection. Overall, the debate usually comes down to two questions: "Is capital punishment wrong?" and "Does it prevent crime?"

Republican Stance

Republicans generally support the death penalty. Many Republicans claim that it is morally acceptable. The thought process is that some crimes are so heinous, horrible or inexcusable that the government should have the authority to completely remove that person from society.

Setting morality aside, Republicans often argue that the death penalty serves a legitimate purpose. They argue that it deters people from killing. The theory is that if the punishment for murder is as severe as death, then people are going to think twice before they kill someone.

In response to a popular argument made by Democrats, Republicans argue that U.S. courts have historically concluded that the death penalty is not "cruel and unusual punishment."

Republicans often argue that the methods used to carry out the death penalty have been adjusted over time to cause as little pain to the subject as possible.

Democratic Stance

Democrats generally oppose the death penalty. They frequently argue that the killing of convicted criminals is immoral. In their eyes, the death penalty is actually vengeance disguised as justice. They argue that in a civilized society, the punishment for murder should not be murder.

Setting morality aside, Democrats also argue that research does not prove conclusively that the death penalty actually does deter crime. They argue that life in prison is an equally effective deterrent as the death penalty. They also say that a life sentence without the possibility of parole saves the state money in the long run, because it costs less to lock up convicted criminals for life than to spend years in the court system trying a capital case and appealing the death sentences.

In addition, Democrats often argue that capital punishment is prohibited by the United States Constitution, which forbids "cruel and unusual punishment." They argue that death itself is cruel and unusual punishment, and that many of the methods used to carry out the death penalty (such as lethal injection) are also cruel and unusual.

The Economy

*This section discusses taxes, job creation,
and the middle and upper class in America*

Brief History of the Issue

At the forefront of every election in the United States is the issue of the economy. Politicians from both parties attempt to hit home with voters as they describe their plans to create jobs, make the tax rate fairer, and grow the economy. What makes this a political issue is that it is often the actions that the government takes that determines whether or not these goals are accomplished. It is often the policies (large or small) that the government enacts towards businesses that determine if individuals can get a job, keep a job, or lose a job. Also, tax rates set by the government often directly translate into the amount of disposable income the average American has. American jobs, tax rates, and business regulations are some of the most significant factors that shape the political issue of the American economy.

Republican Stance

One of the most prominent policies argued by Republicans on the issue of the economy comes from the theory of supply-side economics, sometimes referred to as trickle-down economics. The theory is that if the government limits regulations and lowers taxes on businesses, then as a result, businesses will grow and hire more people. With more people getting jobs, they can support their families and buy more things, which helps the economy. In 2012 the Republican Party advocated to "*reform the tax code to allow businesses to generate enough capital to grow and create jobs.*" In addition the Republicans wanted to "*create an environment where adequate financing and credit are available to spur manufacturing and expansion.*" Because of this stance, Republicans are often positively described as "business friendly" while other times negatively described as "the party of the rich."

Democratic Stance

Democrats have a different approach. Generally, Democrats believe that the wealthier Americans, businesses, and corporations (since they have more money) should bear a larger proportion of the tax burden. With the wealthy paying more taxes, Democrats believe that middle class Americans will have more money in their pockets to spend, which will help the economy. Further, if the largest class of Americans (the middle class) has more money to buy things, businesses will need to hire more people to meet the demand.

In addition, Democrats believe in things that might help strengthen jobs that already exist. For example, many Democrats stand firm in their belief in worker's unions to keep the workplace fair. Another prominent Democratic idea on this topic is to increase the minimum wage to grow and sustain a healthy economy. Because of their stance on the economy, Democrats are often categorized as "standing for the middle class" while sometimes being negatively painted as "anti-business."

Gay Marriage

This section discusses religious beliefs and equality

Brief History of the Issue

In the past ten years, the issue of gay rights has become one of the most highly debated and controversial issues in United States politics. The debate centers on whether or not gay men and women should be able to get married. Historically, marriage in America was permitted only between a man and a woman. In the late 1990s the Defense of Marriage Act (DOMA) was passed. This Act outlawed gay marriage in the United States at the Federal level. In 2012, DOMA was ruled unconstitutional by the Supreme Court and the decision of whether or not gay couples can get married was left to the individual states. In June of 2015, the Supreme Court ruled that same-sex couples can officially marry nationwide. This decision makes this topic less ripe for debate, however candidates may still express their views and opinions on the issue in 2016 to gain support from voters.

Republican Stance

Generally, it is the Republican Party that opposes gay marriage. Republicans point out that marriage has traditionally been defined as a union between a man and a woman. They argue that allowing same-sex couples to marry will weaken the legitimate institution of marriage. In addition, they claim that children are more likely to grow up in an ideal environment when raised by a man and a woman, not two men or two women. Some Republicans argue that children raised in a same-sex household will be deprived of the benefits of both a male and female presence during adolescence.

Some Republicans oppose same sex marriage for religious reasons. They often argue that expanding marriage to same sex couples may lead to churches being required to marry gay couples. This would go against the fundamental principles of that religion. They argue that the government should not force them to embrace moral policies that contradict their religious beliefs. In addition, schools may begin to teach children that same sex marriage is equal to opposite sex marriage—something that many religious Republicans reject.

Democratic Stance

Democrats, on the other hand, generally argue that same sex couples should have all of the same marriage rights as straight couples. They argue that it is fair for same sex couples to be able to celebrate and memorialize their relationships in the same way that straight couples can (through marriage). Advocates of same sex marriage also argue that gay marriage will not harm family values. These advocates commonly argue that there is a lack of data to support the argument that gay marriage will have a negative effect on heterosexual families and that a nation with a diverse range of family types is positive for our society.

Heterosexual married couples receive some benefits from the government such as federal tax benefits, retirement benefits, employee benefits, legal benefits, benefits relating to death, and immigration benefits. Therefore, another popular argument among gay marriage supporters is that gay couples should also have the right to these government benefits. In their view, anything less is discrimination.

Some Democrats argue that the Equal Protection Clause of the United States Constitution grants gay couples the right to get married. The amendment says, "No State shall make or enforce any law which shall abridge the privileges or immunities of citizens of the United States; nor shall any State deprive any person of life, liberty, or property, without due process of law; *nor deny to any person within its jurisdiction the equal protection of the laws.*"

GLOBAL WARMING AND ENVIRONMENTAL POLICY

This section discusses environmental science, skepticism, and the economy

Brief History of the Issue

Global warming, or "climate change" is the idea that the earth's temperatures rose in the 1800's as a result of industrialization. In short, as countries began to build more things (cars, factories, buildings) emissions from the manufacturing of these things caused the earth's temperature to change. Climate change is a unique environmental challenge because it doubles as a *political and an economic issue.* This is because we rely heavily on energy sources that emit carbon dioxide, which is said to be a cause of climate change. Some experts on climate change project that if countries continue to emit carbon dioxide at the current rate, without regulation or a switch to alternative energy sources, climate change could create major and unpredictable problems for us as a species.

The issue of climate change has created a great deal of political tension. On the one hand, voters are driven by their sense of obligation to protect the environment; and on the other hand, voters feel the heavy economic burden of the various policies and proposals designed to do exactly that.

Republican Stance

The Republican Party has historically opposed the theory of global warming. Republicans are skeptical of global warming studies because they believe that they contain errors and because certain groups who stand to gain financially are sometimes behind these studies. In addition to their skepticism, Republicans argue that government policies that are meant to prevent global warming have negative effects on businesses and the economy. This often includes less manufacturing, fewer jobs, and a less efficient economy. Also, some Republicans cite scientific studies that either reject the claims of global warming altogether, suggest that humans are not the cause of it, or suggest that global warming is not a considerable threat.

Democratic Stance

Democrats generally support government global warming programs because they believe in the science behind global warming. For the most part, Democrats place more importance on the issue of global warming than Republicans generally do. In the 2012 election, the Democratic Party discussed climate change more often than the Republicans. Democrats commonly argue that we have a responsibility to future generations to protect the planet we live on by taking the proper precautions. In recent years, Democrats have promoted legislation to limit the amount of harmful emissions produced by manufacturers (referred to as Cap and Trade legislation) and improved fuel efficiency standards as a means to address the global warming issue.

GUN CONTROL

*This section discusses the Second Amendment,
individual rights, and government regulation*

Brief History of the Issue

The issue of gun control (the right to bear arms) comes
directly from the text of the Second Amendment to the U.S.
Constitution, which reads:

> *A well regulated Militia, being necessary to the security of
> a free state, the right of the people to keep and bear Arms,
> shall not be infringed.*

You will notice that the Amendment is neither direct nor is it particularly detailed in its language. As a result, the meaning of the Second Amendment and how it should apply today is open to interpretation. This places a burden on today's politicians and lawmakers to interpret the Amendment and pass laws (or not pass laws) based on those interpretations. Historically, the Amendment has allowed Americans to own—and in some states, carry—guns by obtaining a legal permit to do so. The issue of gun control centers mostly around disagreement over what the Second Amendment (which was ratified in 1791) should be interpreted to mean today.

Republican Stance

In general, Republicans support the right for Americans to keep and "bear" arms. In other words, many Republicans believe that Americans should have the right to buy, own and carry firearms. Many Republicans argue that allowing citizens to own and carry firearms deters crime. The argument is that many violent crimes committed with firearms are committed by people who acquired their gun illegally (without a permit). They believe that a system that prevents law-abiding people from purchasing guns legally and for their own protection puts them at a higher risk from criminals. As a result, laws should empower responsible citizens to defend themselves. These responsible citizens are also not likely to misuse their guns or use them to commit crime.

Republicans argue that in situations such as the shootings in Newtown, CT, Aurora, CO and Columbine, CO, it is a good thing for law abiding citizens to carry guns because it will help to prevent these types of tragedies.

A significant source of controversy surrounding the gun control debate is whether or not high-powered rifles or "assault rifles" should be allowed under the traditional right to bear arms. Many Republicans believe that the Second Amendment includes higher-powered guns and rifles such as shotguns and assault rifles because nothing in the Amendment specifically says that you can't own these guns. Conversely, some Republicans and Democrats agree that the sale of assault rifles and ammunition should be regulated. The two parties disagree, however, on how much regulation is appropriate.

A common criticism of guns is that they might end up in the hands of criminals or the mentally unstable. While both parties agree that nobody wants guns falling into the wrong hands, Republicans frequently argue that psychological evaluations and proper regulations would be sufficient to prevent that from occurring. They argue that completely depriving Americans of guns in an effort to achieve this goal is not only unnecessary, but also dangerous and unconstitutional.

Finally, a common argument and basic philosophy of those who support the right to bear arms is that this country was created in response to an oppressive government (the British King). An armed society would help to prevent any government oppression in the future.

Democratic Stance

Members of the Democratic Party, on the other hand, put forth the following arguments: permitting the right to own and carry firearms increases crime because a gun is more likely to be used for offensive purposes than defensive purposes. In addition, more citizens carrying and owning guns will not increase the safety of citizens, but will actually make altercations more dangerous because people are likely to use a gun if they have it. Another common argument is that gun ownership among citizens makes those who do not own or carry guns feel less safe, and that crime prevention should be left to police. On this point, many Democrats argue that individual citizens lack the training necessary to safely own and operate guns. The police, on the other hand, are trained and experienced with firearms.

Another common argument is that Second Amendment rights have limits and must be considered in light of changing circumstances. They argue that as time has passed and technology has advanced, guns have become much more powerful than they were in the 1700s. The argument is essentially that the Amendment does not explicitly mention the right to carry concealed handguns or assault rifles. Democrats believe that the

Founding Fathers could not have anticipated the power of some of the guns that exist today when they drafted the Amendment. Therefore, the Amendment could not possibly be interpreted as granting everyday citizens the right to own assault rifles.

And finally, in regard to the contention that an armed society would help to prevent government oppression in the future, some Democrats point out that no amount of handguns, shotguns and assault rifles in the hands of the citizenry would be sufficient to defend against the U.S. government's current military might.

HEALTHCARE

*This section discusses Obamacare, its impact,
and the American healthcare debate*

Brief History of the Issue

Perhaps the most highly debated issue of recent times is healthcare. Due to constant policy changes directed towards healthcare and the general complexity of the issue (past and present) we will do our best to lay out the relevant history on healthcare and what both major parties believe should be done.

Traditionally, the U.S. has followed a system of individuals insuring themselves through various private insurance companies. This is in contrast to other nations, many in Europe, for example, where the government pays for a significant portion of an individuals' healthcare costs. Two important terms you may have heard in the healthcare discussion are Medicare and Medicaid. Legislation passed in 1965 set up these two programs. We will begin here.

Medicaid is a federally-established program created to cover those considered to be "low income." Depending on the state you live in, the administration and coverage you may receive will be different. Medicaid helps low income individuals by covering things like doctor visits (sometimes with a small fee for the individual), but does not cover things like prescription drugs or preventive care.

Medicare is a program created for older Americans to ease the burden of increased medical procedures and a lower income that typically comes with age. Medicare is a federal program with standard rules across the country. It covers Americans sixty-five and older and is run through your Social Security office. There are various parts to Medicare: Part A (which covers things like hospital stays), Part B (which pertains to doctor visits, equipment, patient needs, and some therapy), and Part D (which covers partial costs on prescription-type meds). It's important to be familiar with Medicare and Medicaid in the overall discussion on healthcare.

Both parties agree that these programs had significant problems: they didn't provide enough coverage, they sometimes cost the American taxpayer in areas in which they were designed to save money, and millions of Americans did not have any healthcare coverage. These were the main talking points when President Obama and the Democrats pushed for and passed the Affordable Care Act (ACA, also known as Obamacare) in 2010.

Going back to the Clinton administration, Democrats began to support different versions of a healthcare overhaul. During the Clinton White House, the first lady helped create ideas on how to change healthcare policy in the United States. No major changes were actually made at that time. However, this did set the stage for the changes to come.

Obamacare is a hotly debated issue within U.S. politics. *Not one Republican* in Congress voted for the passage of the bill. Various parts of the ACA took effect as early as 2010. The issue continued to face opposition from Republicans in Congress, to the extent that it even caused a government shutdown at one point. In late 2013, the government introduced Healthcare. gov as the website where Americans could sign up and enroll for government healthcare plans provided under the ACA. The website faced numerous administrative and technical problems at its launch, generating even more skepticism from the ACA's opponents. It's likely that Republicans and Democrats will continue to go back and forth on this issue, because elements of the ACA are set to take effect for years to come.

Republican Stance

As discussed, Republicans opposed the passage and implementation of the ACA. Republicans in Congress voted over forty times to defund, dismantle, or repeal the law. These votes were mostly symbolic considering Democrats controlled the Senate and the White House at the time. Generally, Republicans focus on five major points for why they believe Obamacare is not the solution to America's healthcare issue. Their main points are that Obamacare:

- Increased healthcare costs
- Causes insurance premiums to rise
- Diminishes the quality of healthcare
- Added nearly $570 billion in tax hikes
- Adds over $500 Billion to the national debt

In general, Republicans pointed out that the law was too complex and would create future problems for insurance companies; that the law was very expensive and would add a significant amount to the national debt; and would hurt business in America by way of tax hikes and the new obligations for businesses to comply. It's certainly true that Republicans consistently opposed the ACA. However, it is important to note that Republicans were not against improving America's healthcare system. A main critique of the Republican stance towards the ACA was the Republicans' lack of a viable alternative to address healthcare policy in the United States.

Democratic Stance

During President Obama's first term in 2008, he began to build support for an overhaul of the healthcare system. Democrats argued that the ACA was necessary because of the large number of Americans who lacked health insurance and had no access to healthcare. The ACA promised to:

- Provide tax cuts to small business to help offset the costs of employee coverage
- Provide tax credits to help families pay for insurance
- Lower costs for families, businesses and the Federal government
- Reduce our deficit by more than $1 trillion in the next two decades alone

Again, the ACA was designed to provide healthcare for the millions of uninsured Americans and to alleviate many of the financial burdens that Medicare and Medicaid placed on the U.S. government. While there were several Democrats who did not vote for initial passage of the ACA in 2009, the Act was essentially seen as the stance of the Democratic Party for years to come.

IMMIGRATION

This section discusses border security and citizenship

Brief History of the Issue

The United States is a unique country because it was founded entirely by immigrants. The majority of Americans can trace their family lineage back to when one of their ancestors came to the United States from another country. This makes the political issue of immigration an especially challenging one. The term "illegal immigrant" or "undocumented worker" is used to describe people who are unlawfully living in the United States and are not citizens. The Pew Foundation estimates that there were approximately 11.2 million such unauthorized immigrants in the United States in 2012. More than half of them lived in these six states: California, Texas, Florida, New York, New Jersey and Illinois. According to Pew, undocumented workers account for more than five percent of the labor force in America, and as much as ten percent of the labor force in some states. Pew estimates that approximately half of all undocumented workers come from Mexico.

Democrats and Republicans agree that people want to come to the U.S. for a better life. However, lawmakers are challenged with handling several issues (education, healthcare, jobs, border security) relating to immigration and what to do with immigrants who are currently living here illegally.

Republican Stance

Republicans tend to make *border security* the priority when it comes to discussions of immigration reform. As mentioned earlier, illegal immigrants usually enter America through gaps in the U.S. borders, most notably from Mexico. For this reason, some Republicans have proposed using surveillance drones, building a wall, increasing patrol presence, and/or installing cameras to secure the border. They believe that strong border security is necessary to keep the country safe. Republican policy makers often argue that poor border security leads to problems like increased drug trafficking, gang violence, and possibly terrorism within the United States.

Republicans are also concerned about illegal immigration because it leads to people living within the United States who cannot fully participate in society by voting, paying taxes, registering for the military draft, etc.

It's also worth noting that Republicans have tended to oppose amnesty (the idea of granting citizenship to those already in the U.S. illegally) because they believe it could possibly encourage even more individuals to come here illegally in the future.

Democratic Stance

In recent years, Democrats backed policy that addressed the large amount of individuals living in the U.S illegally. In 2012, their platform stated they supported:

> ...[getting] undocumented immigrants out of the shadows, requiring illegal immigrants to get right with the law, learn English and pay taxes and to get on a path toward citizenship.

Like their Republican counterparts, Democrats maintain that the country's current immigration system is "broken" and that our borders should be secured. But they also argue that in order for the U.S. to reform its immigration policies, lawmakers must first address the large numbers of undocumented individuals already living in the country. They say this would do two things. First, it would give the country a fresh start towards any future immigration policy reform; and second, it would allow those undocumented individuals who have already established their lives and families in the U.S. the ability to stay. This stance in the immigration debate is sometimes referred to as *amnesty*. Before being granted the right to apply for citizenship, Democrats would require these individuals to admit that they are in the country illegally, pay a penalty and taxes, and learn English.

One aspect of the Democrats' immigration policy is a plan to address young people who were brought to the United States illegally when they were children, a population the Democrats often refer to as "DREAMers." The DREAMer nickname comes from a piece of bi-partisan legislation called the DREAM Act, which is an acronym for *Development, Relief, and Education for Alien Minors*. The DREAM Act, which has been proposed but has not yet passed due to a lack of Republican support, would allow these young people a path to citizenship after completing two years of college or serving two years of military service with an honorable discharge.

National Security/
Terrorism

*This section discusses security, the right
to privacy, and basic human rights*

Brief History of the Issue

Almost everyone would agree that one of the basic purposes
of government is to keep the country and its citizens safe.
Both Republicans and Democrats agree that we must protect
the nation, but they sometimes disagree on what is the most
effective way of doing so. What makes this issue particularly
complex is that Republicans and Democrats do not have a clear

"platform" on national security. Decisions regarding the safety of the nation are often made in light of the circumstances, not on political ideology. These circumstances typically raise questions like:

- *Should we go to war?*
- *Should we maintain an alliance with this country or that country?*
- *Should we take an aggressive stance abroad, or keep to ourselves?*
- *How do we combat terrorism?*
- *How much money should we spend on our military?*

Due to this complexity, we will approach this section from a different angle by highlighting the most common positions taken by Republicans and Democrats in response to the most pressing problems associated with keeping our country safe.

Military Spending

When it comes to the amount of money that America spends on its military, Republicans are more likely to support increases and reject proposed decreases than their Democratic peers. Republicans generally take the position that a large and powerful military will keep us safe, both before we are attacked and if we are attacked. A large military will scare enemies from attacking us because of the strength of our military. In addition, if we are attacked, a large and powerful military will enable us to fight our enemies quickly and effectively. In short, many Republicans believe that spending a lot of money on our military is worth it.

Democrats, on the other hand, generally support reducing the amount of money that we spend on our military. They take the position that our military is big and powerful enough as it is. Our military is unquestionably the largest of any country, and is capable of handling any threats that would challenge the size and might of our armed forces. Many Democrats argue that we should spend less money on our military and instead focus on things like rebuilding the economy. In addition, many Democrats place their confidence in our alliances with other countries to help keep us safe and fight terrorism abroad.

International Conflicts

An international conflict could stem from a number of different things: an oppressive foreign government, genocide, a hostile dispute between two countries that has resulted in warfare, a foreign political crisis, terrorism, or piracy. It is important to note that these conflicts may or may not directly involve the United States. When conflicts like these arise, it is usually Republicans who suggest the use of the military as a solution.

Many Republicans take the position that the United States, as the global superpower, has a responsibility to protect and promote freedom and democratic values around the world through the use of the U.S. military. Republicans are more likely to call on the military to handle conflicts abroad when U.S. interests are involved. These interests usually include national security, economics, or promoting freedom and democracy.

Democrats, on the other hand, are more likely to suggest diplomacy, negotiation, and the procedures of the United Nations as a solution to international conflicts. Democrats generally take the position that the U.S. should not be the "world police." They argue that this is too expensive and puts our troops at an unnecessary risk. In addition, Democrats generally believe that conflicts are resolved more effectively through the cooperation and joint efforts of many nations.

Domestic Surveillance

After the 9/11 terrorist attacks, a Republican majority in Congress drafted the PATRIOT Act. This legislation approved the use of wiretaps, surveillance, and various searches to prevent future acts of terrorism. The issue here is that some searches that became permissible under this Act are at odds with the Fourth amendment to the U.S. Constitution, which guarantees *"the right of people to be secure in their persons, houses, papers and effects, against unreasonable searches and seizures."*

Republicans received considerable criticism from Democrats regarding the PATRIOT Act. Democratic critics argued that our Fourth Amendment rights are guaranteed by the Constitution and the threat of terrorism does not justify the government violating those rights by spying on its citizens. Despite this criticism, however, Democrats have continued this controversial practice, using the same reasoning as Republicans—that it is necessary for protecting the homeland against terrorist attacks. It is unclear whether or not one party will change its position on this issue in the 2016 election.

However, at least partial reform of the country's domestic surveillance activities occurred in mid-2015 with the passage of the USA Freedom Act, which dramatically limited the government's ability to collect phone records in bulk. It also increased transparency of the national security court that directs the government's data collection efforts. The USA Freedom Act was supported by the vast majority of Democrats in the House and Senate, but it sharply divided Republicans in both chambers. Therefore, it's possible that the Republican Party will have quite a bit of difficulty reaching a consensus on domestic surveillance as they hammer out their 2016 Presidential platform.

Guantanamo Bay

After the invasion of Afghanistan in 2001, the United States set up Guantanamo Bay detention center in Cuba to house terrorist suspects who were captured. Republicans have defended this facility, arguing that detaining and interrogating suspected terrorists is an effective and necessary method of defeating terrorism. They argued and continue to argue that the information obtained through interrogations helps us defeat terrorist organizations, and has led to many successful missions.

Democrats have argued and continue to argue that this facility is unethical and should be closed. They claim that Guantanamo Bay hurts our international image and that it is a violation of basic human rights. They condemn "enhanced" interrogation and torture as immoral, and argue that the United States should be above these actions. Currently, Democrats have kept the facility open in recent years while releasing a significant percentage of its prisoners. Republicans object to those releases, declaring that many of the prisoners who have been released have returned to their ranks as terrorists and continue to fight and plot against the United States. Democrats counter that surveillance indicates that the vast majority of released prisoners have not re-engaged in terrorist activities.

At the time of this writing, there are reports that the Obama administration will make a renewed push to close Guantanamo Bay before Obama leaves office.

ADDITIONAL ISSUES

The issues that follow are distinct from those in the previous section in the sense that they are not traditionally viewed as partisan matters. In other words, these topics will be heavily discussed on the news, in the media and in debates, but opinions about them don't usually fall along party lines like they do with abortion or defense spending.

Our goal here is merely to make you aware of a few of the important issues you're likely to hear about in the prelude to the 2016 Presidential election. We'll give you a little history on each one, as well as some of the major points and opinions, and let you watch how it all plays out in the election.

CAMPAIGN FINANCING

Ever since George Washington bought drinks for his pals in the lead up to Election Day, money in politics has been a contentious topic in Presidential campaigns. Whether it's about requiring union workers to make political contributions in order to keep their jobs, or the practice of billionaires and corporations donating undisclosed amounts of money to benefit their favorite candidates, campaign finance reform is one of those things politicians often talk about but rarely act upon.

Back in the 1970s, policymakers passed the Federal Election Campaign Act (FECA), which paved the way for the Federal Elections Commission (FEC). The FEC is charged with supervising and enforcing the regulations that govern campaign spending, as established by FECA. But ever since its inception, FECA has faced legal challenges from donors and political parties on the grounds that certain elements of the Act are unconstitutional in that they violate the donors' First Amendment right to free speech. They have alleged (often successfully) that money equals speech and therefore cannot be regulated by the government; and in some cases, that corporations have the same right to free speech in this context as individual people do. This means that generally speaking, a corporation's right to spend money on certain aspects of political campaigns cannot be limited because to do so would violate the First Amendment. The most famous case of this type was *Citizens United v. Federal Election Commission,* which was decided by the U.S. Supreme Court in 2010.

Many have expressed fear that the *Citizens United* ruling would lead to a tsunami of unlimited special interest money in campaigns, thereby diminishing the integrity of the political process. They have called for a complete overhaul of the campaign finance system. But since reforming the system would require the efforts of the elected officials themselves— the very recipients of those billions of dollars in campaign contributions—it is not surprising that there hasn't been a groundswell of movement toward that end.

Currently, Republicans and Democrats both accept large donations from major corporations, special interest groups, and other contributors. It's unclear if and when a movement to end these types of campaign influences will occur, and which party (or candidate) will take the lead.

EDUCATION

There are several aspects of public education that are likely to be debated in the 2016 election. They are:

Common Core

Common Core is a set of math and language arts standards for what all K–12 students in the nation should have learned and be able to demonstrate by the end of each grade. The goal was to establish uniform educational benchmarks and assessments across the country. States can choose whether or not to implement Common Core. Some people and organizations oppose the standards on the notion that they promote a "national curriculum" that by-passes state and local authority over public education. Others say that the standards don't take into account differences in culture and learning styles, and that they stifle creativity. Still others say that the initiative's focus on math and language arts leaves little to no time for other subjects, and that the tests are too difficult and stressful for students and teachers alike. Proponents say Common Core levels the playing field and raises standards for all students in America, regardless of where they attend school.

Teachers' Unions

Teachers' unions have been in existence since the 1850s. Their original purpose was to promote teaching as a profession, and to advocate for teachers in the political arena. As time went by, the unions became the voice for teachers in collective bargaining. More recently, Federal programs such as Race to the Top and others have impacted long-standing union protections such as tenure and pay based on seniority. There has been a shift toward performance-based evaluation of teachers, meaning that policymakers are making efforts to link teacher pay to student achievement. There is quite a lot of disagreement among all stakeholders on this issue.

School Choice

Traditionally, public school children in America have been assigned to a particular school (a neighborhood school) based on residential boundaries. But in the 1980s there began a movement called school choice in which parents were given the option of using public funds in the form of "vouchers" to send their children to the private, religious or charter school of their preference. Alternatively, in some states parents receive tax credits for tuition to an out-of-district or private school. Opponents of school choice say that this practice drains public schools of much-needed funding, negatively impacting the children who remain. Some fear that the non-traditional schools lack oversight. Still others say that diverting public funds to religious schools runs contrary to the division between church and state. But school choice supporters argue that parents should have the right to educate their children as they see fit, and that parents should not have to send their child to a failing school just because it's in their neighborhood. Many believe that a voucher system leads to greater competition among schools to deliver a quality education, thereby attracting more students and essentially shutting out underperforming schools.

School Funding

In the U.S., individual states set the funding amounts for public schools within their boundaries. This money comes from the state budget and also from local property tax revenue. In 1973, the Supreme Court established that it is legal for school funding to be based upon property taxes, even if it leads to unequal funding from one state or school district to the next. Some states have mandated that the funding for all schools be the same regardless of the wealth or poverty in the district. Others spend more per pupil in affluent districts than they do in poorer districts. In still others it's the opposite— poor districts are given more money per pupil than those of their wealthy neighbors. Consequently, there have been calls for the states with the greatest funding disparities to overhaul their school funding formulas.

THE ISLAMIC STATE

The Islamic State in Iraq and al-Sham, also known as ISIS, IS and ISIL, is an offshoot of the terrorist organization al Qaeda in Iraq. In 2013, ISIS broke from al Qaeda and began a violent push to establish an Islamic caliphate (a type of Islamic government) across the Middle East and gain authority over all Muslims worldwide, whether they like it or not. Since then ISIS has taken over large swaths of Iraq and Syria, including the control of major cities and oil fields in both countries. While the exact number of ISIS fighters is unknown, it is estimated to be in the thousands and includes sympathizers from Europe, the United States and the Arab world, among others.

ISIS has become known for its savage treatment of hostages, civilians, and prisoners; treatment that has included beheadings, burning alive, and mass executions. Western journalists—some of whom were American—were beheaded and videos of their murders were posted online, along with threats to carry out even more killings if the U.S. and its allies didn't back off.

These atrocities prompted President Obama to authorize air strikes against the militants beginning in June 2014. The United States was joined in these offensives by allies around the world. In February 2015, Obama sought to expand America's efforts to defeat ISIS by asking Congress for an Authorization to Use Military Force. Although Congress has approved funds for the ongoing air strikes, at the time of this writing they have failed to debate or vote on that authorization. Some Congressional Democrats have been reluctant to act on the issue because they want to limit the number of troops and have a firm deadline for an end to the conflict—two things the authorization does not guarantee. Some Republicans have been reluctant to push for the authorization because it does not allow for the use of ground troops. They also believe that the President already has the power to use military force, so the authorization is unnecessary.

With no quick end to the ISIS threat in sight and no apparent will on the part of Congress to come up with a bipartisan response, this issue will certainly be a ripe topic for debate in the 2016 Presidential campaign. Note that we discussed more broadly the issue of international conflict and terrorism in our previous section on national security.

Marijuana

Marijuana is a well-known drug in the United States. So well-known that in 2013, half of American adults admitted to at least trying marijuana in their lifetime. However, the fact remains that even though marijuana has been decriminalized in some states, it is still illegal at the federal level to possess, use, and sell it. What makes marijuana a political issue is the fact that many Americans believe it should not be illegal (the pro-legalization crowd).

While it's true that Republicans are more likely to oppose the legalization of marijuana, this is not always the case. Similarly, Democrats are often more open to the idea of legalization, but this is also not always the case. Again, this issue is not divided along party lines as much as many others. Generally speaking, those who advocate for the legalization of marijuana (regardless of their party affiliation) argue that legalization of the drug will create a taxable good that can be carefully regulated if under government control. This would be an improvement from the current reality, which is that money is put into the hands of drug dealers who frequently sell the product to consumers. By regulating marijuana, taxpayers will spend less money fighting a "war on drugs" while at the same time generating taxable income. In addition, many supporters argue that marijuana is less dangerous than various products that are already legal, such as cigarettes and alcohol. Generally, the supporters of marijuana legalization argue that the benefits of keeping marijuana from society are not worth the overall costs.

Conversely, those who advocate for the continued laws against marijuana use argue that marijuana has a detrimental effect on the individual and therefore society as well. Legalizing the recreational use of marijuana could have certain negative effects within society. They argue that drugs are dangerous not only to the person using them, but also to others. For example, people may smoke marijuana and get behind the wheel, which would subject others to their dangerous behavior. Also, marijuana can sometimes be considered a gateway drug:

individuals first use marijuana and then move on to other harsher drugs such as cocaine or heroin.

Still, decriminalization of marijuana at the state level appears to be a trend that shows no signs of fading away. The 2016 Presidential candidates will most certainly be asked whether they're in favor of decriminalization at the Federal level as well.

Race Relations

Our nation has a long and difficult history in regard to race relations. As a young nation, our society faced trying times, such as the institution of slavery, Jim Crow laws, and segregation in the South. Throughout our history, America has also persevered. The Civil War was, in part, a noble effort with the objective of ending slavery in America. The Civil Rights movement, along with landmark cases such as *Brown v. Board of Education,* effectively ended racial segregation, and today, we have our first African American President. However, racial tension has nevertheless remained a contentious issue in America.

Recent events have brought this subject into national headlines: the shooting death of Trayvon Martin, an unarmed black youth, by an armed Florida neighborhood watch volunteer named George Zimmerman; the police shootings of an unarmed black man in Ferguson, Missouri named Michael Brown; Tamir Rice, a black pre-teen from Cleveland who was shot while playing with a toy gun; Walter Scott, who was shot in the back in Charleston, North Carolina; and the deaths of other black males who were in police custody at the time, most notably Eric Garner in New York and Freddie Gray in Baltimore. These incidents, along with a string of others across the country, have prompted widespread marches and protests among black community members since the last Presidential election, some of which became violent. From these demonstrations came the slogans "Black Lives Matter," "I Can't Breathe," and "Hands Up, Don't Shoot."

In response, the U.S. Justice Department launched investigations into several of the affected law enforcement agencies to determine if there had been a pattern of institutional racism and civil rights violations within them. In some of those investigations, it was concluded that there had been such violations and patterns of abuse.

In the 2016 Presidential election, the strained relationship between minorities and law enforcement will likely be discussed at length, and the candidates will have to describe their proposed solutions to the problem.

VOTER INFORMATION

We want you to be totally prepared for Election Day, so before we close out *POLITIGUIDE 2016*, we'd like to give you some general information about voting. Read on to learn about registering to vote, what to expect on Election Day, and alternatives to traditional voting.

How to Register

To vote in the U.S. Presidential general election, you must:

- Be at least eighteen years of age
- Be a U.S. citizen
- Meet your state's residency requirements
- Be registered to vote

There are several ways you can register to vote. You can **register by mail** by picking up a voter registration form at a public library, public school, or city or county clerk's office. You'll simply fill out the form and send it in according to the instructions on the document. In most states there are two kinds of forms available—a state voter registration form and the National Mail Voter Registration Form (NMVRF), which you can also download at www.eac.gov/NVRA. Both forms accomplish the same thing, but there are a couple of states and territories that do not accept the NMVRF, and they are listed on the form. You should also not use the NMVRF if you are a uniformed service member; in that case you should register using the Federal Post Card Application available at www.fvap.gov.

Alternatively, you can **register in person** at your local Department of Motor Vehicles, a state or local voter registration or election office, military recruitment offices, public assistance and state-funded disability agencies, and any other state-authorized voter registration agency.

Finally, in some states you can **register online**. To find out if your state offers this option, contact your State or local election office.

Regardless of which voter registration alternative you choose, you will have to present documents proving that you are who you say you are. Although registering to vote is usually easy, make sure to begin the process well in advance of Election Day just in case. Each state has deadlines for registering, so don't miss that cut off or you won't be able to vote. After registering, the U.S. Election Assistance Commission recommends that you contact your State or local election office to confirm your voting eligibility at least seven weeks before the election. That way if there is a problem, you'll have enough time to correct it and complete your registration.

Your voting location—or *polling place*—is assigned to you based upon your address. Be sure to find out the location of your polling place well in advance of Election Day, and always remember to update your voter registration when you move.

What to Expect on Voting Day

Once you have confirmed that your voter registration is in good standing, you should identify your polling place and voting hours on Election Day. If you registered to vote by mail, be sure to take along some documentation just in case you're asked to verify your identity. Your valid driver's license; a bank statement, paycheck or utility bill with your name and address on it; and your citizenship papers (if you are a naturalized citizen) should suffice.

In most jurisdictions, the local election office sends all registered voters a sample ballot a few weeks in advance of

Voting Day. You'll likely be surprised at how many races, referendums and amendments are on the ballot in addition to the Presidential race.

Plan to arrive at your polling place early and be prepared to stay awhile if the lines are long. Once inside, you'll be directed to one of several election volunteers who will check to make sure your name is in the registration records. They may also ask to see documentation proving your identity if this is your first time voting. Then they'll hand you your ballot (if you live in a state that uses paper ballots, that is) and you'll either stand in another line or go directly into an available voting booth.

- If you are given a **paper ballot**, you'll use either a paper punch machine to indicate your votes, or you'll mark your votes by filling in ovals or making checkmarks with a pencil or pen. Once you're done, you'll take the ballot out to another volunteer who will have you drop it into a box or feed it into a scanner which will read your vote and preserve your ballot.
- If your state uses **electronic voting equipment**, just follow the directions on the voting machine inside the booth.
- If you have any questions, don't hesitate to ask one of the volunteers. In our experience, they're always very eager to help.

Alternative
Ways to Vote

If you arrive at the polling place and your voter registration cannot be verified for some reason yet you believe you are entitled to vote, you should request a ***provisional ballot***. This is a special ballot that allows you to go ahead and cast your vote on Election Day even if your registration is in question. An election official will then review your eligibility after the polls have closed, and if it is verified, your vote will be counted.

If you know that you're not going to be able to make it to your polling place on Election Day or if you simply don't want to brave the potential lines, you have a couple of options. Many jurisdictions offer ***early voting*** in the days or weeks leading up to an election. With early voting, you simply go to a designated location (usually an election office but it can also be some other special voting site, such as a library) and go through the same procedure as if you were voting the usual way. Your ballot will then be set aside and counted along with all the others after the polls close on Election Day. You can also vote by filing an ***absentee ballot***. Some states will only let you use an absentee ballot if you meet specific criteria for why you can't vote on Election Day. Others will let you file an absentee ballot for any reason. Contact your local election office to inquire about absentee ballots and early voting.

www.politiguide2016.com